3-D Shapes

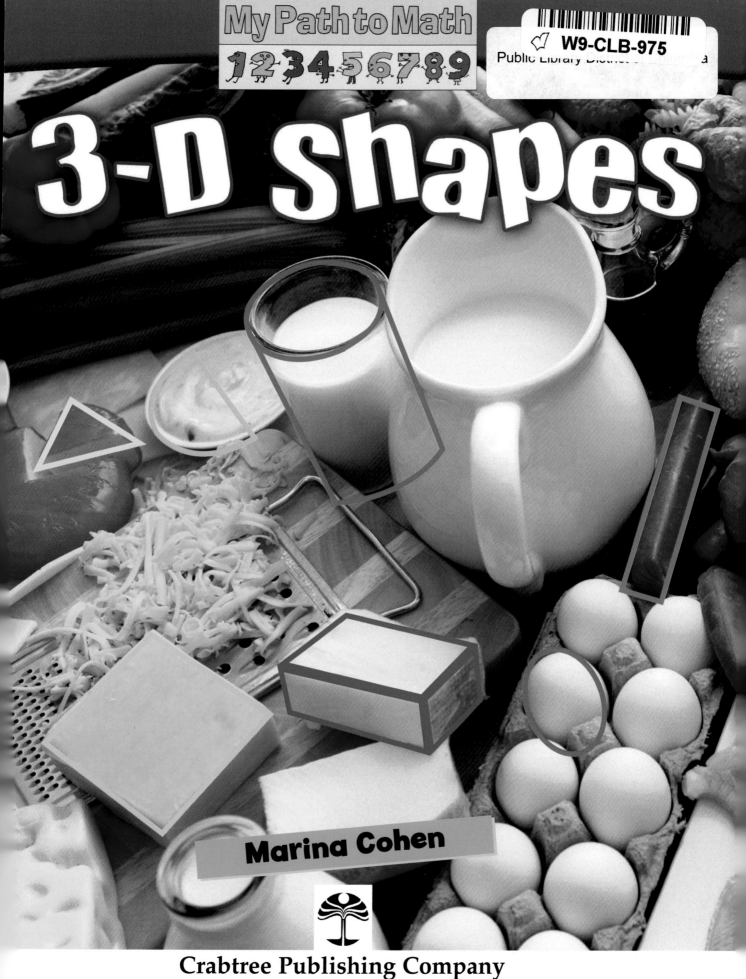

Marina Cohen

Crabtree Publishing Company

www.crabtreebooks.com

Author: Marina Cohen
Publishing plan research and development:
 Sean Charlebois, Reagan Miller
 Crabtree Publishing Company
Editor: Reagan Miller
Proofreader: Crystal Sikkens
Editorial director: Kathy Middleton
Project coordinator: Margaret Salter
Prepress technician: Margaret Salter
Coordinating editor: Chester Fisher
Series editor: Jessica Cohn
Project manager: Kumar Kunal (Q2AMEDIA)
Art direction: Cheena Yadav (Q2AMEDIA)
Cover design: Kanika Kohli (Q2AMEDIA)
Design: Divij Singh (Q2AMEDIA)
Photo research: Ekta Sharma (Q2AMEDIA)

Photographs:
Istockphoto: Igor Vesninov: p. 12 (right)
Photolibrary: Brand X Pictures: p. 11;
 Coll-Francisco Cruz: p. 21
Q2A Media: 4, 5, 6, 10, 11, 12, 13, 14, 16, 19, 21, 23
Other images by Shutterstock

Library and Archives Canada Cataloguing in Publication

Cohen, Marina
    3-D shapes / Marina Cohen.

(My path to math)
Includes index.
ISBN 978-0-7787-6779-4 (bound).--ISBN 978-0-7787-6788-6 (pbk.)

    1. Shapes--Juvenile literature. I. Title. II. Series: My path to math

QA445.5.C64 2010   j516'.156   C2010-900819-7

Library of Congress Cataloging-in-Publication Data

Cohen, Marina, 1967-
    3-D shapes / Marina Cohen.
      p. cm. -- (My path to math)
    Includes index.
    ISBN 978-0-7787-6779-4 (reinforced lib. bdg. : alk. paper) --
    ISBN 978-0-7787-6788-6 (pbk. : alk. paper)
    1. Shapes--Juvenile literature. 2. Supermarkets--Juvenile literature. I. Title.
    II. Series.

    QA445.5.C644 2011
    516'.156--dc22

                                        2010003027

Crabtree Publishing Company

Printed in the U.S.A./062016/JF20160505

www.crabtreebooks.com   1-800-387-7650

Published in Canada
Crabtree Publishing
616 Welland Ave.
St. Catharines, ON
L2M 5V6

Published in the United States
Crabtree Publishing
PMB 59051
350 Fifth Avenue, 59th Floor
New York, New York 10118

Published in the United Kingdom
Crabtree Publishing
Maritime House
Basin Road North, Hove
BN41 1WR

Published in Australia
Crabtree Publishing
3 Charles Street
Coburg North
VIC, 3058

Contents

A Trip to the Grocery Store

Justin loves to go to the grocery store. He pushes the cart. He helps his mother find food. The grocery store is a great place to hunt for shapes!

Some shapes are plane shapes. A **plane** shape is flat. It has two **dimensions**. The length is one dimension. The width is the second dimension. You can **measure** the length and width of a plane shape.

Activity Box

Plane shapes are also called 2-D shapes. The 2-D stands for "two dimensions." Can you name these 2-D shapes?

length

width

rectangle

length width

circle

Every shape has length and width.

Three Dimensions

Mom tells Justin that other shapes are **solid**. Solid shapes have three dimensions. You can measure the length and width. You can also measure the height.

Shapes with three dimensions are also called 3-D shapes. These shapes have **faces**. They most often have **edges** and **corners**, too. The faces of a 3-D shape are the flat parts. The edges are the parts where the faces join. The corners are the points where the faces meet. A corner can also be called a **vertex**.

parts of a 3-D shape

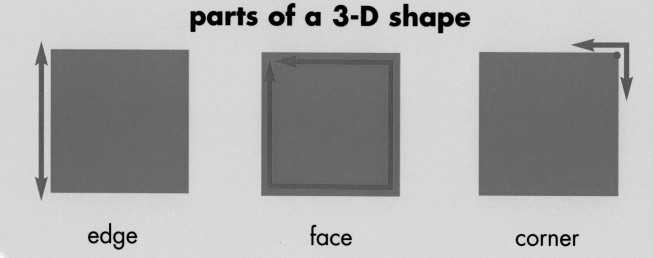

edge   face   corner

A loaf of bread is a 3-D shape.

height

length

width

Sweet Spheres

Mom asks Justin to help her pick a bag of oranges.

An orange looks like a ball. A ball is a 3-D shape called a **sphere**. A sphere has no edges and no corners. These shapes have just one face. The face goes all around the sphere!

The objects shown below have a sphere shape.

Activity Box

Can you think of other objects that are spheres?

Objects with 3-D shapes can be piled.

Food Cubes

Justin and his mother visit the deli counter. The man at the deli counter offers them a piece of cheese. The cheese is cut into **cubes**.

Justin's mother says that a cube is a 3-D shape. It has six square faces. The faces are of **equal** size.

A cube has twelve edges. It has eight corners.

Activity Box

1. Draw a square.

2. Draw another square.

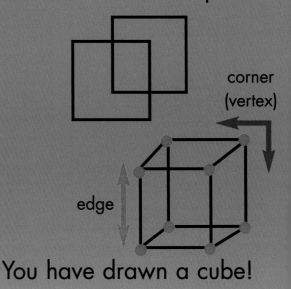

corner (vertex)

edge

3. Join the two squares using lines like this.

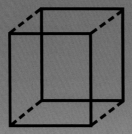

You have drawn a cube!

The bottom of a cube is a face, too!

cube

corner
(vertex)

face

edge

Cylinder Shapes

"How about soup for dinner?" Justin asks.

"Help me find a can of soup," Mom says.
"We also need a roll of paper towels.
Soup can be messy!"

They find the can and the
towels. Both things have
the same shape.

Mom explains that the can and towels are
cylinders. A cylinder has two edges and
no corners. A cylinder has three faces.
It has a flat face on each end. The
third face connects the flat faces.
The third face circles the shape.

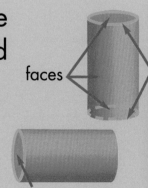

faces

face

Activity Box

Use a pencil and paper to trace the **net** on page 13.
Cut out the net. Roll the rectangle into a cylinder.
Fold down the circles on the ends.

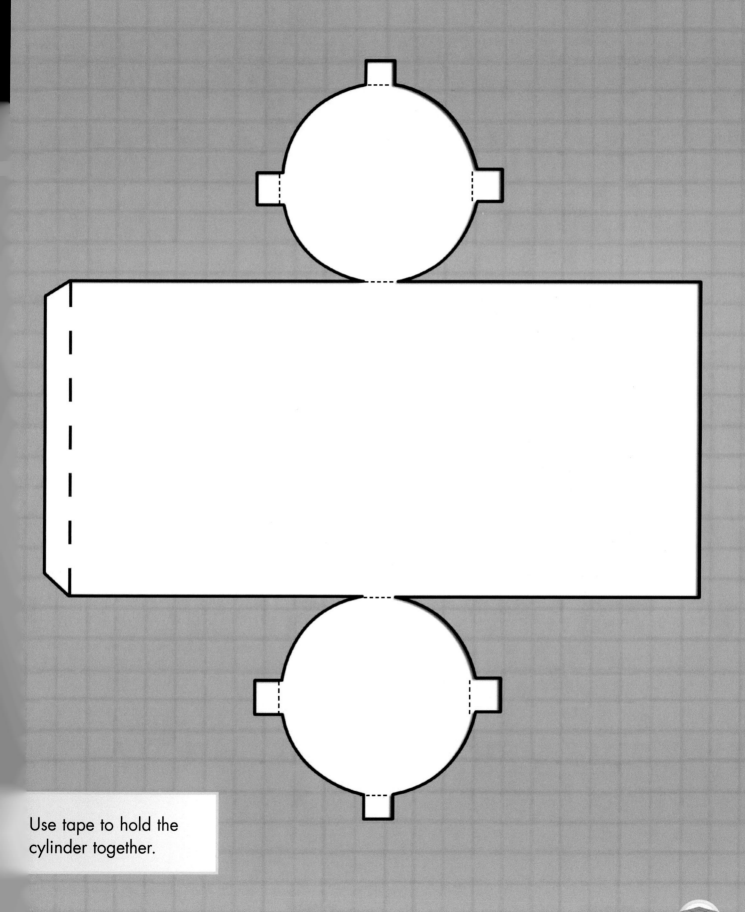

Use tape to hold the cylinder together.

Cones Come in Handy

Oh, no! There is a spill on the floor! Justin and his mom see an orange **cone** shape on the floor near the spill. The cone warns people not to walk there.

A cone has two faces. One of the faces is a round, flat circle. The second face goes around the circle. It connects the circle with the corner at the other end. A cone has one edge and one corner.

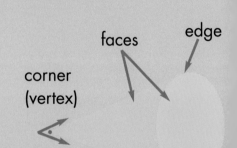

faces

edge

corner (vertex)

Activity Box

Draw this shape on construction paper. Then cut out the shape. Roll the shape into a cone. Then turn the cone into a magician's hat! You can decorate your hat with stars, moons, and glitter.

ice-cream
cone

**CAUTION!
WET
FLOOR**

Can you think of other
kinds of cones?

Building Pyramids

Justin and his mom go to the bakery. Justin sees a tasty piece of cake. The cake has berries piled on top. The berries form a **pyramid**.

The pyramid of berries has five faces. One of the faces is its **base**. A base is a face that a shape can sit upon. This pyramid has a square base. Its four other faces are triangles.

A pyramid that has a square base has five corners. There are four corners around the bottom. There is one corner at the top. This kind of pyramid has eight edges.

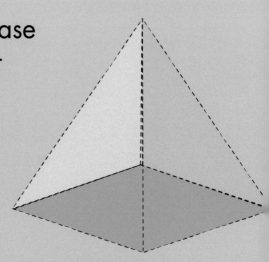

Activity Box

Use blocks or books to build a pyramid.

There are five faces—
four sides plus one base.

pyramid

triangle sides

square base

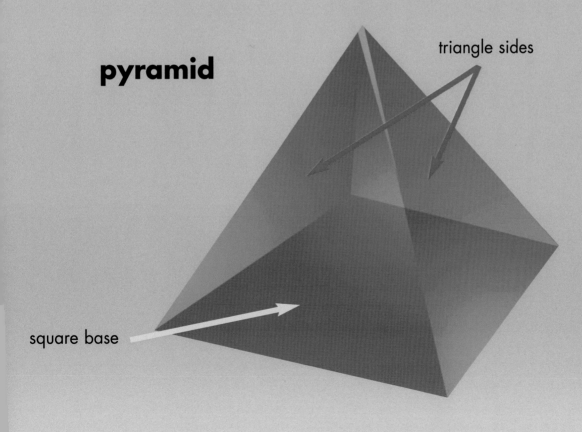

Rectangular Prisms Are Everywhere!

Justin sneezes into his sleeve.

"Bless you," says Mom. "I almost forgot. We need tissue!"

Justin picks up a box of tissue. It has a small rectangle on each end. The ends are connected by four long rectangles. Mom says the box is a **rectangular prism**.

Count the faces of a tissue box. There are six. There are eight corners and twelve edges.

Activity Box

Get a pen and paper. Have someone time you. Walk around your house. Write down all the rectangular prisms that you see in five minutes.

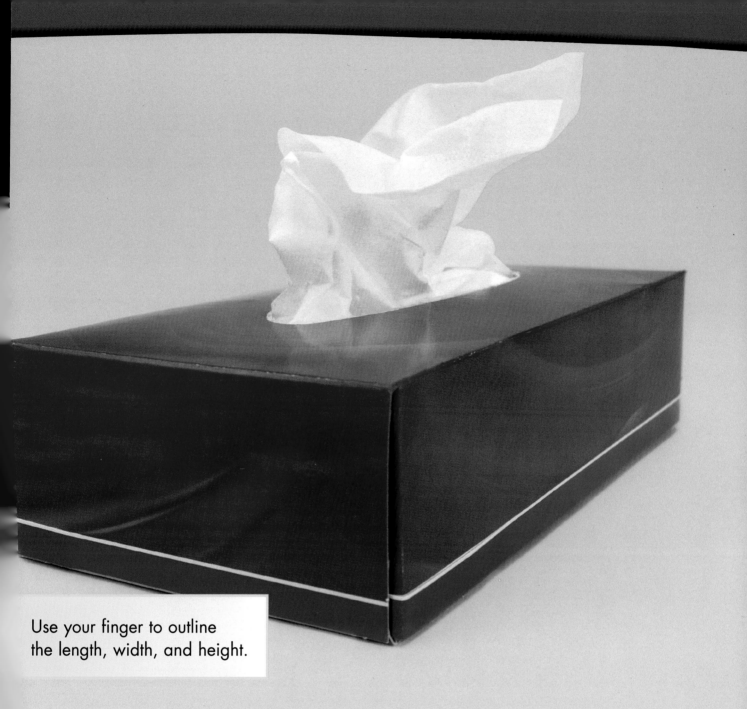

Use your finger to outline the length, width, and height.

rectangular prism

rectangular faces

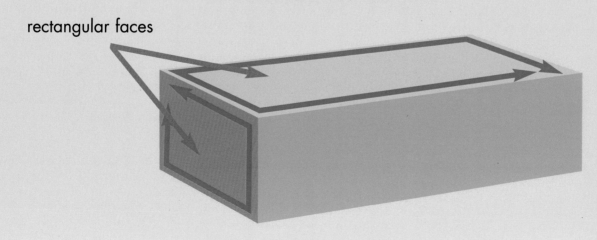

Triangular Prisms at the Checkout

At the checkout, Justin and his mom place groceries on the belt. The belt moves the groceries forward. But first, they must place a bar on the belt. The bar separates their groceries from other people's groceries. The bar is another kind of prism. It has a triangle on each end. It is called a **triangular prism**.

This kind of prism has five faces. Two of the faces are triangles. The other three faces are rectangles. A triangular prism has six corners.

It has been fun hunting for shapes at the grocery store. Now it is time to go home.

Activity Box

Help unpack groceries in your house. Look for the 3-D shapes Justin has learned about.

20

rectangle-shaped face

triangle-shaped face

triangular prism

Every item on the belt has a shape.

triangular prism

Glossary

base A face that is a shape's bottom

cone Solid shape with a base that's a circle and sides that meet at one point, or vertex, at the top

corners More than one vertex, the points where surfaces meet

cubes Solid shapes with six square (and equal) faces, twelve edges, and eight corners

cylinders Solid shapes with bases on each end that are circles and a curved surface that joins the bases

dimensions Different ways of taking measure, such as length, width, and height

edges Places where two surfaces join together

equal Alike in size, measure, or amount

faces Flat surfaces of solid shapes

measure Finding out the size or amount of something, such as how tall, how long, or how heavy something is

net Flat shape that can be folded to make a 3-D shape

plane A flat surface

pyramid Solid shape with triangles for sides, can have a square or triangle as a base

rectangular prism Solid shape with two small, alike rectangles on each end connected by four long retangles

triangular prism Solid shape with two alike triangles on each end connected by three rectangles

sphere Solid shape that is perfectly rounded like a ball

solid A shape that has length, width, and height

vertex A "corner," a point where faces or lines meet

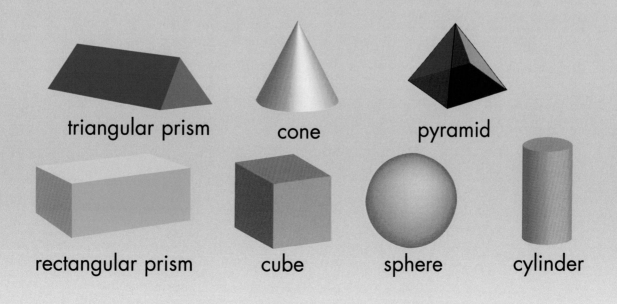

triangular prism   cone   pyramid

rectangular prism   cube   sphere   cylinder

Index